The Wrong Letter

Alan MacDonald

Illustrated by Judy Brown

One morning the postman came down
Elm Road. In his bag were two letters.
They looked like this:

There were two Miss Jones in Elm Road. Pippa Jones lived at number 10. She was mad about ponies.

Flo Jones lived at number 79. She was mad about football. But that morning the postman had broken his glasses and he couldn't see very well. That's how the mix-up began.

Pony-mad Pippa was out at the stable when her letter came. Pippa had a pony called Blossom who was a champion jumper. She gave Blossom some oats and a kiss on the nose.

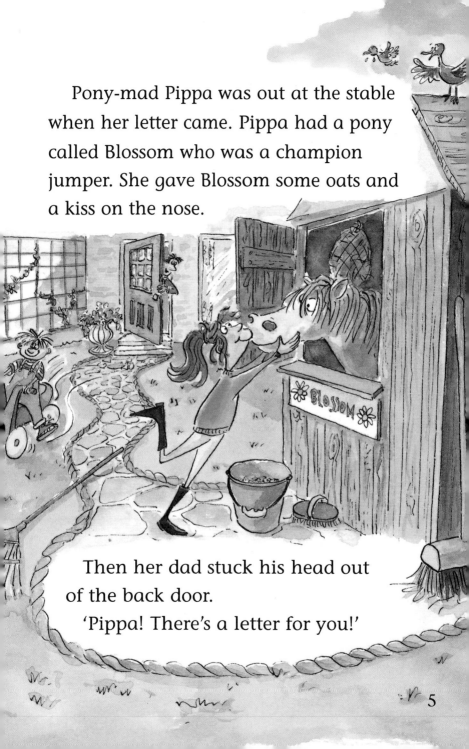

Then her dad stuck his head out of the back door.

'Pippa! There's a letter for you!'

Football-mad Flo was in the garden when her letter arrived. Flo played for Redland Rovers. She was wearing her Rovers kit as usual. She dribbled past the cat and swerved round the swing.

'Thud!' the ball hit the back door. 'Goal!' cried Flo.

'Flo!' called her mum. 'Stop that racket
and come inside. There's a letter for you.'

Flo tore open her letter.

It said:

Dear Miss Jones
The Junior Cup is on Saturday
at Chestnut field.
We hope to see you there.

'Wow!' said Flo. 'I'm playing in the
Cup Final on Saturday. Redland Rovers
will win for sure.'

At 10 Elm Road, Pippa was also
reading her letter.

Dear Miss Jones,
The Junior Cup Final is on Saturday at
Redland Park. We hope to see you there.

'Fantastic!' said Pippa. 'I'm riding
Blossom in the Junior Cup. We're sure
to win.'

Pippa and Flo couldn't wait for
Saturday to come. They didn't notice
that they had got the wrong letter.
They were both going to the wrong
place.

On Saturday morning Pippa rode
Blossom to Redland Park.

Down the road they passed Flo on
her way to Chestnut Field.

Pippa stared at Flo in her red and white football kit.

'Fancy dressing up like that to play a stupid game of football,' she thought to herself.

Flo stared at Pippa in her black riding hat and boots.

'Fancy dressing up like that to ride a boring old pony,' she thought to herself.

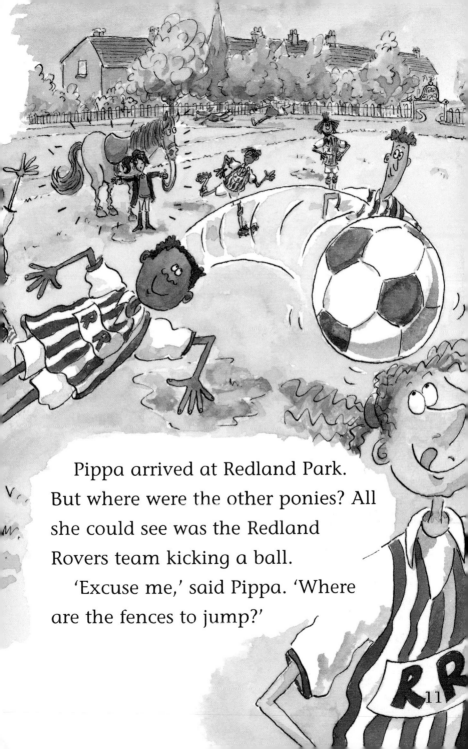

Pippa arrived at Redland Park. But where were the other ponies? All she could see was the Redland Rovers team kicking a ball.

'Excuse me,' said Pippa. 'Where are the fences to jump?'

The Rovers team laughed.

'This is a football match. Ponies can't play,' said one.

Rovers' captain went over to Pippa.

'Have you seen Flo Jones? She hasn't come yet and we're one player short.'

'I don't know anyone called Flo,' said Pippa. 'My name is Pippa Jones.'

'Well, you'll have to play then,' said
the captain. 'Hurry up and get
changed. Kick-off is in five minutes.'

Pippa was horrified. She didn't want
to play football. She wanted to ride
Blossom in the Junior Cup. She tried to
explain but the Rovers team didn't
listen.

They pushed her into the changing room. They gave her football boots and a shirt. The shirt came to her knees and the boots pinched her feet. When Pippa ran she kept tripping over her laces.

They lined up for kick-off and the referee blew his whistle to start the game.

The ball came whizzing towards Pippa.

'What shall I do with it?' she wailed.

'Just kick it that way,' shouted Rovers' captain.

Pippa kicked the ball.

'Youch! My toe!' she yelled.

The ball went to one of the Blue team. Pippa tried to get it back. But she tripped over her laces and fell in a muddy puddle.

'This is all a mistake!' moaned Pippa. 'I'm in the wrong place!'

Flo was in the wrong place too. She
was in Chestnut Field. But where
was the Cup Final? All she could see
were girls trotting round on ponies.

'What's all this?' Flo asked a man
in a brown hat.

'It's the Junior Show. I'm Mr Trotter,
one of the judges. What's your name?'

'Flo Jones. I'm here to play football.'

Mr Trotter wasn't listening. He was busy looking at a list of names.

'Ah yes, here you are. Miss Jones. You're jumping twenty-third.'

'Jumping? Me?' Flo turned pale. 'But I can't... I haven't even got a pony.'

Mr Trotter laughed. 'Dear me! You've come without your pony? Then we'll have to find one for you.'

Five minutes later Flo was sitting on a big, black pony. It snorted and stamped its feet.

'His name's Thunder. You have to show him who's boss,' said Mr Trotter.

Flo looked at Thunder. She was pretty sure he was boss.

'I don't know how to ride,' she said.
'There's been a mistake…'

'You'll be fine. Good luck!' said
Mr Trotter and slapped Thunder on the
back. Thunder galloped off with Flo
holding on tight. The fences looked
very high. Flo wanted to jump off but
Thunder wouldn't stop.

The loudspeaker boomed:
'And the next rider is Miss Pippa Jones on Thunder.'

The crowd clapped.

'But my name isn't Pippa!' cried Flo. 'Somebody get me down!'

It was too late.

Thunder was heading for the first fence. Flo shut her eyes. She was sure they were going to hit it.

Just in time
Thunder jumped. They landed with a
bump and Flo's hat slipped down over
her eyes. Now she couldn't see where
she was going.

Thunder sailed over the next jump.
And the next. But Flo was slipping out
of the saddle. She was almost upside
down, hanging onto Thunder's neck.

'What an odd way to ride,'
said Mr Trotter.

Thunder took the next three fences
at a gallop. They came to the last one,
a high brick wall.

Thunder took off. 'He-elp!' cried Flo,
flying in the air.

They landed with a
thud. Then Flo fell off onto the grass.

Everyone crowded around her.
They picked her up and patted her on
the back.

'Are you all right?'

'Well done.'

'Jolly good riding.'

'What happened?' asked Flo,
getting up.

'You won. You jumped all the fences
in the fastest time,' said Mr Trotter.

He pinned a rosette on Thunder and
gave Flo a silver cup.

'This year's winner of the Junior Cup
is Miss Pippa Jones,' he said.

'My real name is Flo,' smiled Flo
happily.

4

Back at the Cup Final, things weren't
going well for Pippa. Her legs hurt. She
was wet and muddy and the boots were
killing her. There were two minutes left.
The score was 2–2, but Pippa didn't
care. She just wanted the game to end
so that she could go home.

The Blues' goalkeeper kicked the ball
out. It bounced straight to Pippa. She
wasn't pleased to see it.

'Go away!' she shouted crossly
and gave the ball a mighty kick.

To her surprise the ball soared
through the air towards the Blues'
goal. The goalkeeper dived – but
the ball hit the back of the net.

'Goal!' shouted the Rovers.
'What a goal!'

At that moment the final whistle blew. Pippa was Girl of the Match. Her team carried her off the pitch, cheering.

Everyone wanted to pat her on the back. Pippa had won the Junior Cup for Rovers.

After the game Pippa set off home with Blossom. On her way up Elm Road she passed Flo.

Pippa and Flo both stopped. They both stared. Both of them were covered in mud and holding silver cups.

'Is your name... Pippa Jones?' asked Flo.

Pippa nodded. 'Then you must be Flo Jones.'

Then they understood. So that's what had happened.

'I must have got *your* letter,' said
Flo. 'I went to a pony show.'

'And I must have got *your* letter,'
said Pippa. 'I went to a football match.'

They both started to laugh.

'Football is fun,' grinned Pippa,
'when you get used to it.'

'And riding a pony is really quite
exciting,' said Flo.

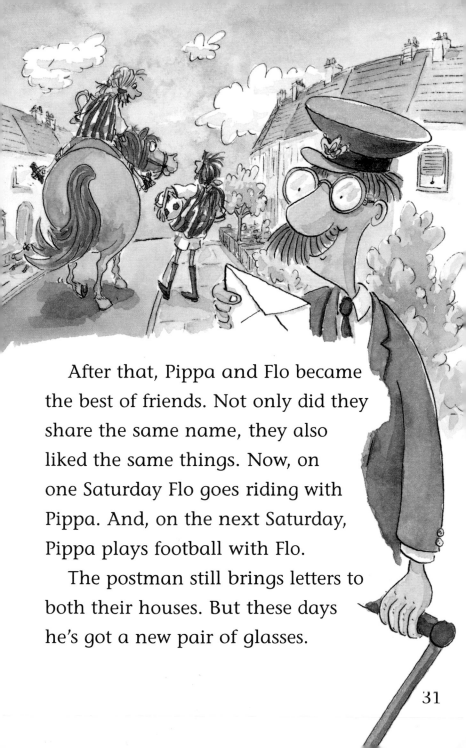

After that, Pippa and Flo became the best of friends. Not only did they share the same name, they also liked the same things. Now, on one Saturday Flo goes riding with Pippa. And, on the next Saturday, Pippa plays football with Flo.

The postman still brings letters to both their houses. But these days he's got a new pair of glasses.

About the author

I write for children because
I like making up stories. Some
of my stories are in books
while some have been on
radio or television.

I live in Nottingham with
my wife and three children.
Sometimes we all make up
stories together at bath time.

I was once sent a wrong letter myself.
It asked me to go to London to collect a
prize for one of my radio plays. The only
trouble was I hadn't written the play! There
was another writer called Alan MacDonald
and I'd been sent his letter by mistake.